The Perfect Gift
of Quiet Celebration

Friendship

This is a STAR FIRE book

STAR FIRE BOOKS
Crabtree Hall, Crabtree Lane
Fulham, London SW6 6TY
United Kingdom

www.star-fire.co.uk

First published 2007

07 09 11 10 08

1 3 5 7 9 10 8 6 4 2

Star Fire is part of The Foundry Creative Media Company Limited

The CIP record for this book is available from the British Library.

ISBN: 978 1 84451 945 3

Printed in China

Thanks to: Chelsea Edwards, Cat Emslie, Victoria Lyle,
Sara Robson, Gemma Walters and Nick Wells

The Perfect Gift
of Quiet Celebration

Friendship

Daisy Seal

Foreword

I sit here in my beautiful cottage garden,
surrounded by grazing animals, birds in song and
the heady aroma of gorgeous flowers in full
bloom. Of course, such a wonderful, intoxicating
concoction has offered the inspiration for this
series of books which reflect on the values
underlying the best of our relationships:
generosity of spirit, kindness and love.

Daisy Seal

When you hold my hand, I feel warmed by a thousand friends.

You know that I will always be with you, even if we don't see each other for months or years.

The value in friendship often seems unremarkable because it is unspoken.

Sometimes, when I
think of you, my heart
bursts with pride.

Your friendship has been tall and strong, as though we were many together facing out defiantly to the world.

Friendship makes us strong.

Friendship, like a humble
bulb, is always there, waiting
for the right moment to appear
and disappear.

*Friends are like petals on
a meadow flower, at once
delicate yet strong.*

Friendships appear swiftly in the heady fertility of Spring.

Your generosity has always come unbidden, and warm, like the mid-summer sun.

Friendship helps you share the good times, as well as the bad!

Focusing on a particular friend can reveal unexpected empathies.

*It is helpful to have a companion
in a stressful environment,
especially when everyone else
seems so competitive.*

Straining for success can stretch the fabric of a friendship. Be careful not to pull too hard.

Friendships can cross all boundaries. A genuine desire for companionship is what matters most, not origin or environment.

A kind word can return with a friend many years later.

*Short term friendships can dissolve
as quickly as the morning dew.
Always pace your relationships.*

*Some friendships last a lifetime,
but it is hard to understand why.
Don't try!*

If you're feeling a little low, you'll find that others feel the same. A good friend will always share your emotions.

*Learn to appreciate the beauty
of a simple friendship.*

*A friendship of the like-minded
is a treasure that will last
a lifetime.*

Some people only find one true friend. That should be more than enough!

Strong friendships can be found in a common appreciation.

If you seek too far afield you
might miss the perfect
friendships around you.

*Friendship is a complex mix of
intimacy and diversity.*

*Your friends will always stand
tall for you.*

*It is much easier to let friendships
grow naturally, than to seek
them too fiercely.*

*Embrace change as a source
of growth and enjoyment in
your friendships.*

*With friendship comes
responsibility, gladly borne.*

A misunderstanding between true friends can be swiftly resolved by gentle but determined contact.

True friendships, being inclusive
and generous, do not exclude
others, but embrace the
humanity in everyone.

*Friendships must allow
everyone to grow at their
own pace.*

A good friend will understand your need for silence.